South Coas[illegible]m the Air

Written and edited by Andrew Bray
Photography by Patrick Roach
Designed and typeset by Caroline Helfer
Charts by Tony Garrett

Front cover: Yarmouth Harbour
Back cover: The Needles

Published by Bray and Roach
Moonfleet Farmhouse, Higher Anstey, Nr Dorchester, Dorset DT2 7PU

ISBN 0-948788-26-7

Copies of any of the photographs appearing in this book may be obtained from Patrick Roach, Moonfleet Farmhouse, Higher Anstey, Nr Dorchester, Dorset DT2 7PU

Whilst every care has been taken over the compilation of this book, neither the authors nor the publishers can be held responsible for any errors or omissions or for any mishaps arising from its use

Origination by Positive Colour Ltd, Maldon, Essex.
Covers printed by Clifford Frost Ltd, London.
Printed and bound by Scotprint Ltd, Musselburgh, Scotland.

South Coast from the Air

Aerial views of the coastline, harbours and rivers of the South Coast from Anvil Point to Beachy Head

Andrew Bray and Patrick Roach

Contents

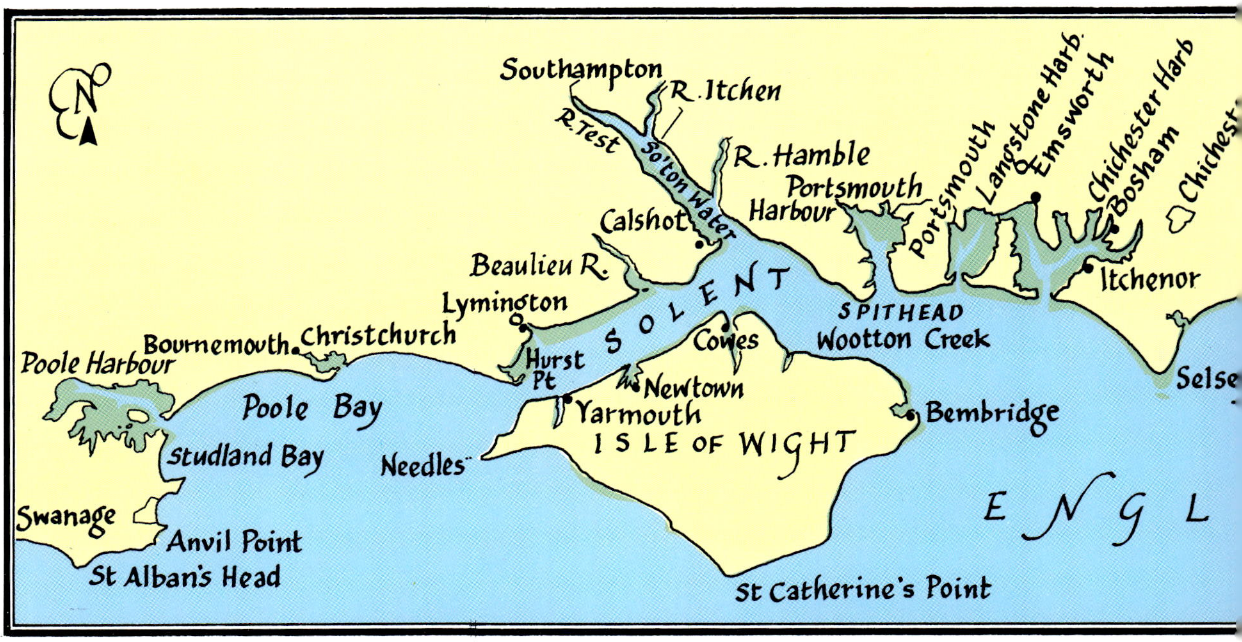

N
Southampton
R. Itchen
R. Test
So'ton Water
R. Hamble
Portsmouth Harbour
Portsmouth
Langstone Harb.
Emsworth
Chichester Harb
Bosham
Calshot
Beaulieu R.
Itchenor
Lymington
SOLENT
SPITHEAD
Cowes
Wootton Creek
Bournemouth
Christchurch
Poole Harbour
Hurst Pt
Newtown
Selse
Poole Bay
Yarmouth
Bembridge
Studland Bay
Needles
ISLE OF WIGHT
Swanage
Anvil Point
St Alban's Head
ENGL
St Catherine's Point

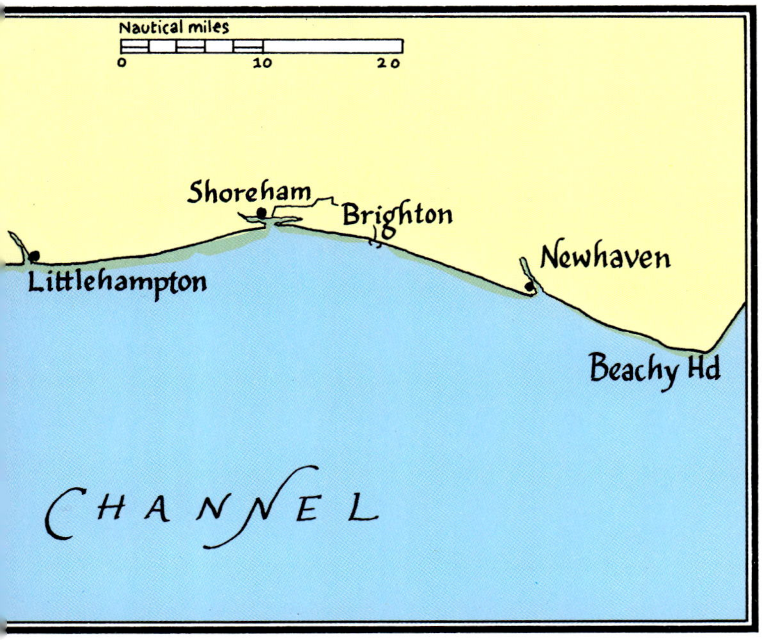

Overleaf: On a clear day...Christchurch looking towards Hengistbury Head, the Needles, Hurst Point and, at the top left, the Solent

Chapter 1

Introduction

The waters between Anvil Point and Beachy Head are the most popular sailing grounds of the United Kingdom. From Poole Harbour in the west and Newhaven in the east many thousands of small craft are moored and sailed for pleasure. In particular, the sheltered waters of the Solent are home to many who cruise for pleasure in craft from dinghies to ocean-going yachts, and race from club level right up to the top international events such as Cowes Week and the Admiral's Cup.

Left: Old Harry looking towards Swanage. The visibility in this picture is fairly typical with a light haze. Most of the photographs were taken at between 500 and 800 feet

Left: Poole Harbour from Parkstone. The Town Quay is at the centre left of the picture with Holes Bay and Cobbs Quay at the top right. The visibility here is very much better for photography than that in the picture above

The idea for this book came about as a result of the many aerial photography sorties I have flown with Patrick Roach for *Yachting Monthly*, in particular for their popular and successful Classic Passages series. Together we have flown at low level over most of the coastlines of Northern Europe, from the German Frisian Islands down to the River Vilaine in South Brittany as well as covering the English coast from Land's End to South Foreland and as far north as the River Ore.

After our first few flights we both realised the added perspective that aerial views offered of the coastline, ports and harbours and the value they have for anyone sailing those waters. Apart from being useful to help visualise a particular harbour or hazard, they allow the reader better to relate place with place more easily, to orientate himself, which is not always easy when following a narrow channel or curving coastline. They give a feel for distance, show hazards both coastal and offshore and, of course, give a unique and uncluttered view of ports and harbours.

We cannot claim in any way to be the first to use aerial photography in this way. I remember back in the 1960s a series of booklets produced by Castrol covering much the same ground and many pilot books now use pictures from the air. Peter Bruce's

Left: The Needles. One of our private goals was the get clear photographs of the wreck of the *SS Varvassi* which lies about 100m to the west of the light – the results can be seen on page 43

Below: Beaulieu River and Buckler's Hard. To give an idea of the perspective offered by aerial photography, Southampton Water is clearly visible at the top of the picture

excellent books *Solent Hazards* and *Wight Hazards* (Boldre Marine Ltd) also use aerials to good effect. What I believe we have achieved is to produce a comprehensive book, most of it in colour, covering the harbours, approaches and entrances between Anvil Point and Beachy Head and containing some of the best aerial pictures taken of the South Coast.

We have not concentrated only on the hazards, nor is it intended that this book should in any way, replace pilot book or chart. However, reproducing low water pictures alongside those taken at high water gives a very good feel for a particular harbour entrance or river. The real value of the pictures is that they offer a clear view of these waters, bridging the gap between chart and reality. It is often very difficult to envisage a place from the two dimensions of a chart and, whilst sea or land level photography is a help, only from the air is it possible to build up a complete picture.

Taking the pictures

If it sounds easy just to hop into a plane and snap off a few rolls of film, I can assure you that the real story is somewhat more complicated. Detailed planning is necessary in order to 'catch' the tidal windows in the right order, and then one has to be able to arrange the weather. It's not just the sun that's needed, it is also the visibility, and all too often, when you have the sun in high pressure weather, there is heavy haze, perhaps not apparent on the ground but

Above: The entrance to the River Hamble at LW showing Hamble Spit and the extent to which this 'Bond Street of yachting' has been taken over by marinas and moorings

very obvious from the air. The ideal is shortly after the passage of a cold front, and many hours were spent grounded waiting for promised fronts to come through.

Three flights were made to take the low water pictures at equinoctial springs and a further three to get the high water photographs. As any South Coast sailor will know, high water springs here typically occurs at around noon and midnight, with low water at 0600 and 1800, when it was either still dark or the low sun caused too many reflections to be able to see the banks and hazards clearly. In the event, the best pictures were obtained on 30th September, 1988, a few days after the equinoctial tides but when there was still a range of 3.7m and the Portsmouth LW height was 1.0m, fairly typical of a normal spring tide. A further flight on 6th April, when the heights were 0.2m and 4.8m at Portsmouth, show the best low water detail, though unfortunately the weather was less accommodating. All low water pictures were taken within an hour of LW and high water pictures two hours either side of HW.

Planning the pictures, the weather and tides apart, was a complex business. When you're travelling at between 80 and 100 knots the harbours come at you thick and fast and there is no time to think about the pictures as you take them. Nor is the cramped cockpit of a light aircraft, sitting in the slipstream from an open window, the ideal place to pore over charts.

Our homework had first of all to envisage what pictures would be of most interest and of most use to anyone

navigating these waters. Next came calculations of sun height and angle at the planned time of the picture or sequence of pictures. For example, an early morning picture of the entrance to the River Hamble taken from the west into the sun would show little detail owing to reflections and all the colours would appear flat. We then drew a detailed route on a chart with all the circuits clearly shown and calculated flyover times based on an average aircraft speed of 90 knots, and marked picture requirements along the route. And finally, apart from offering prayers to the weather gods, we copied the chart to a more manageable size for convenient cockpit use.

Of course, it never worked out as planned. A picture missed might mean a second circuit delaying the schedule, the dictates of air traffic control meant that the planned route was not always possible, and there was always the chance of the weather closing in or the visibilty deteriorating.

The first set of low water photographs were taken on 9th September, 1987 (HW

Below: Chichester Harbour entrance at LW. Wherever possible, low water pictures have been published alongside those taken at high tide

4.8m, LW 0.6m), the second on 30th September, 1988, the 3rd on 6th April, 1989, and the final sequence on 28th May, 1989. The time lapse of over 18 months reflects the difficulties in matching tides and weather conditions. In the event our patience was rewarded, because this book has, I believe, the finest collection of pictures of the South Coast contained in a single publication.

The majority of the photographs were taken from a height of between 500 and 800ft, except those taken from over built-up areas, when it was 1,500ft, or more.

Nikon cameras with 50mm and 105mm lenses were used and the colour pictures were taken with Fujichrome film.

Using this book

The aerial pictures depicted offer a greater understanding of the topography of the coastline, harbours and rivers between Anvil Point and Beachy Head than is possible from the chart or pilot book. Whilst in the descriptions of coastal hazards along these coasts some pilotage information is presented, it is not intended in any way that this book should replace conventional yachtsmen's pilot books. Rather it should be used in conjunction with both pilot book and chart, as it allows the navigator to build up a better visual idea of the coastline.

Whilst every effort has been made to ensure the accuracy of information presented here, neither the authors nor publisher can, in any way, accept responsibility for any errors or omissions.

Andrew Bray, October 1989

Above: Birdham Pool with Bosham and Thorney Channels at the top of the picture

Right: Beachy Head Lighthouse looking east

Chapter 2

Anvil to Hurst Point

At Anvil Point the rocky Dorset cliffs give way to the open and more sheltered waters of Poole Bay. Five and a half miles to the south of Poole Harbour and 15 miles to the west of the Needles, Anvil Light is one of the main long range lights on the South Coast and every year welcomes hundreds of vessels sailing across and along the English Channel and in towards Poole.

Swanage and Studland

North from Anvil the coast opens into two large bays, Swanage and Studland, which, although open to the east, offer good shelter to the prevailing westerlies. Yachts waiting for a break in the weather before heading west or across the Channel can gain significant advantage over those in Poole by anchoring in either of these by virtue of the fact that they are both closer to Anvil, the jumping off point, and because they are clear of the fast-running tides in the approaches to and entrance of Poole Harbour. Plans for a marina in Swanage are discussed from time to time and, although the latest proposals had been rejected at the time of writing, if the Bay is developed it will make this town a popular stopping off point for yachts working down-Channel.

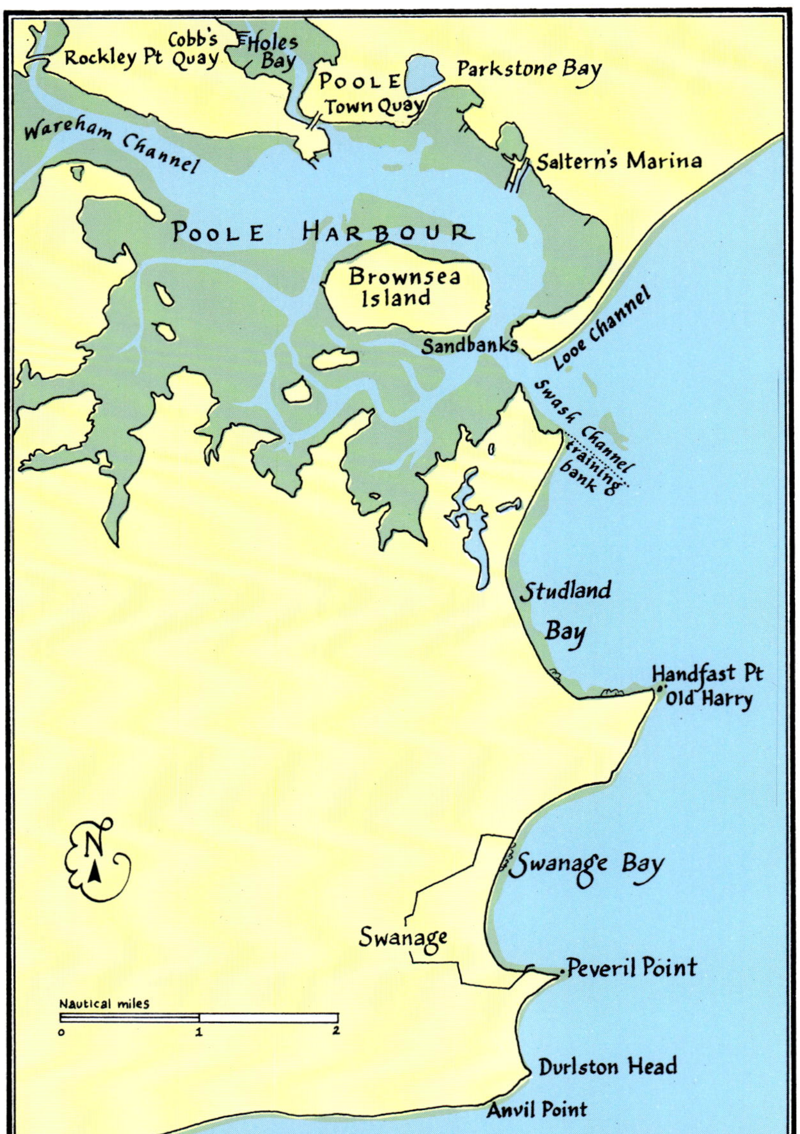

Holding is moderately good in both bays, and whilst Swanage boasts all the amenities of a holiday town Studland has few facilities, although there is a pub within walking distance of the beach and the excellent Studland Hotel. When anchoring in Studland keep about 300m clear of the first two of three prominent projections from the cliff. Both bays, in westerly weather, have some of the clearest water on the South Coast and so are popular with divers. All boat owners are well advised to keep a good look-out for small craft and inflatables flying the blue and white, swallow tailed 'A' flag and give them safe clearance.

Studland has a magnificent swathe of white sand stretching all the way to Shell Bay and the entrance of Poole Harbour and,

Left: Swanage Bay. The best anchorage is to the north and north-east of the pier. The rocky Peveril Ledge can be clearly seen extending out from Peveril Point, its eastern extremity being marked by a small red can buoy. In quiet weather it is possible to pass about 200m inside the buoy. In strong wind against tide conditions overfalls may develop in the race off Peveril which may extend up to ½ mile to seaward of the buoy, especially on the ebb

Above: Anvil Point and Light. There are no offlying dangers close under the cliffs at Anvil and at at some states of the tide favourable eddies may be found inshore. In fresh or strong onshore weather reflected waves can cause confused seas. At the top left of the picture is Peveril Point and beyond Swanage Bay. The two white posts in the centre of the picture are transits marking the eastern end of a measured mile and a similar pair are at the western end

although parts of this may become crowded close to the car park in summer months, landing from a dinghy in offshore weather is possible for its whole length. There is an unusual 'hazard' at Studland, in that it is home to one of the country's longest established naturist colonies. Other types of wildlife also abound amongst the dunes behind the beach.

The main hazards between Anvil Point and Poole Harbour are Peveril Ledge just to the south of Swanage Bay and marked with a red can buoy, shoal water close by the distinctive Old Harry Rocks (Handfast Point), the well marked Training Bank to the west of the Swash Channel and the Poole Bar sands to the east of the Swash. There are tidal races off Handfast Point and, on the ebb, Peveril

Above: Handfast Point and the Old Harry Rocks, with Studland Bay and Poole Harbour in the background. Old Harry and several other stacks have, though erosion of the chalk cliffs, become separated, and at the extreme right can be seen the remains of 'Old Harry's Wife', blown down during a gale in the 1950s

Right: Studland is a popular and attractive anchorage with its long sandy beach. There are rocky outcrops close inshore along the southern side and about 200m off Redend Point at the southwestern corner of the Bay. To the west of Old Harry, seen here at LW, there are outcrops from the cliff and yachts should not anchor within 300m of the most easterly pair because of ledges which show clearly here. Note also the shoal patches extending to the east and south-east of Old Harry. The best anchorage is about 600m north into the Bay and as far west as draught allows

Left: Several banks just inside the entrance dry at LW and the main channel is clearly buoyed and passes to the east of them. Tides can run very fast in the entrance and, apart from the chain ferry, there is frequently the added hazard of angler's boats drifting on the tide. On summer weekends the narrow entrance can become very congested with craft as diverse as ferries and fishing boats to high-speed runabouts and sailboards

Ledge, and in wind against tide conditions overfalls can develop.

Poole Harbour

Except at very LW springs, it is usually safe for yachts of moderate draught coming from the east to pass inside buoy No 3 (green, conical). The Swash Channel is well marked and lit and affords an all-weather entrance to Poole Harbour, although on the spring ebb in a strong southeasterly large seas may build up. Close under Sandbanks, on the east side of the entrance to Poole, is the Looe Channel which offers a valuable short cut, though it should be treated with caution and not attempted near LW, especially at springs, nor on the ebb when there is a strong easterly. The sandbanks here are prone to shift so keep a careful eye on the depth sounder at all times.

Left: The approaches to Poole Harbour are wide and well marked. To the east can be seen the sandbanks of Poole Bar. The yachts on the left are in the main Swash Channel with Shell Bay to their left, just before the entrance. There is an inshore passage, the Looe Channel, just under Sandbanks on the right-hand side of the entrance. In the centre of the picture is Brownsea Island, owned by the National Trust and an important bird sanctuary where landing is prohibited. The chain ferry can be seen on the Sandbanks side of the harbour entrance

Right: The entrance to Poole Harbour on a busy weekend. The Training Bank shows up clearly with Shell Bay just beyond. Yachts must give way to commercial shipping in the main Swash Channel although, except to the immediate south of the western side of the entrance, there is adequate water close outside the channel to the west

With the recent introduction of a new cross-Channel ferry service and the extensive oil exploration and production in Poole, commercial traffic has increased significantly over the last few years. In the narrow approaches to the harbour small craft are required under the collision regulations to give way to ships and there is, for the most part, adequate water just outside the main channel. Anyone visiting the harbour for the first time would also be well advised to keep a good look-out for the chain ferry that plies across the entrance all year round. When departure is imminent, two black balls are hoisted at the 'front' end, and as the tide in the harbour entrance can run very fast, give the ferry a clear berth. In particular, never pass close ahead of or behind the ferry on account of the chains.

Poole claims to be the largest natural harbour in England and one of the largest in the world. Although tidal range is small, the stream runs very fast through the narrow entrance due to the sheer size of the harbour, and also because the double HW causes the tide to stand in the harbour for much of the tidal cycle, as a glance at the tidal curves in the almanac will show. It is also worth noting that some tide tables for

Left: Looking across the harbour towards the entrance and, beyond, Peveril Point. The power boats in the centre left of the picture are in the main channel which has been dredged in recent years to allow deeper commercial vessels to use the Harbour. Although not LW, the sandbanks between the main and Wych Channels are visible. As can be seen, there is no speed limit in the harbour...

Poole Bridge give times of LW because HW cannot be predicted accurately; a fact that has led to many a yachtsman coming unstuck when taking short cuts under the misapprehension that it was HW. There are a number of anchorages (though care must be taken not to anchor close to moorings) in the harbour, though most visiting yachtsmen opt for the Saltern's Marina or the popular Poole Quay, which in summer months gets very crowded and can be uncomfortable in strong southerly winds and because of the volume of traffic plying between the moorings and Cobbs Quay Marina in Holes Bay above the lifting road bridge.

There is plenty of scope for exploration by dinghy in the harbour, which at times can become quite rough, but landing is prohibited on the islands, particularly Brownsea which is an important bird sanctuary. Those with shoal draught boats can explore many parts of the harbour and carry the tide up to Wareham, where there is some space alongside the quay for yachts prepared to take the ground.

Poole is a large town with all kinds of shops, pubs and restaurants, and as a yachting centre has good yards, chandlers and repair facilities.

Above: Poole Harbour with the Salterns Marina in the foreground, Parkstone Bay to the right and the Town Quay just to the left of the two chimneys. To the right of the chimney is Holes Bay and Cobbs Quay, above the lifting Poole Bridge and at the top left of the picture the harbour extends past the Poole Harbour YC Marina and Rockley Point towards the Wareham River

Top: Salterns Marina and Parkstone Bay. There are plans for another marina at Parkstone

Above: Cobbs Quay and Davis's Boatyard

Right: Poole Quay, a very popular destination for South Coast yachtsmen which becomes crowded in summer months. Berths are clearly marked according to boat size, with the smaller being towards the bridge

Above: Poole Harbour YC Marina with the ferry terminal above and the Town Quay to the left. There are regular passenger and freight services to Cherbourg

Left: Looking north across the harbour with Green, Furzey and Browsea Islands. The drilling rig is on Furzey Island with Goathorn Point on the right of the picture, Cleavel Point on the left. Both anchorages here are popular

Right: Wareham Quay, where there is some space for yachts able to take the ground as it dries out at LW

Left: The winding lower reaches of the River Frome which leads off the western end of the harbour towards Wareham

Poole to Hurst Point

Although the direct route from Poole to the Solent takes the yachtsman well offshore, there is adequate water closer inshore for much of the way between Poole and Christchurch with the exception of Christchurch Ledge which runs two miles in a southeasterly direction out from the distinctively shaped and red-coloured Hengistbury Head, marked at its southern end by a south cardinal buoy. Minimum depth over the ledge is around 3m, though a greater hazard is posed by overfalls on the ledge in strong wind against tide conditions and by the large number of pot markers in the vicinity. A good look-out is essential because of this. At the inshore end of the ledge, about 500m off Hengistbury, lie the Beerpan Rocks, and there is a further rocky patch to the south-east of the Head, both of which can be cleared by staying about 600m off. Between Hengistbury and the entrance

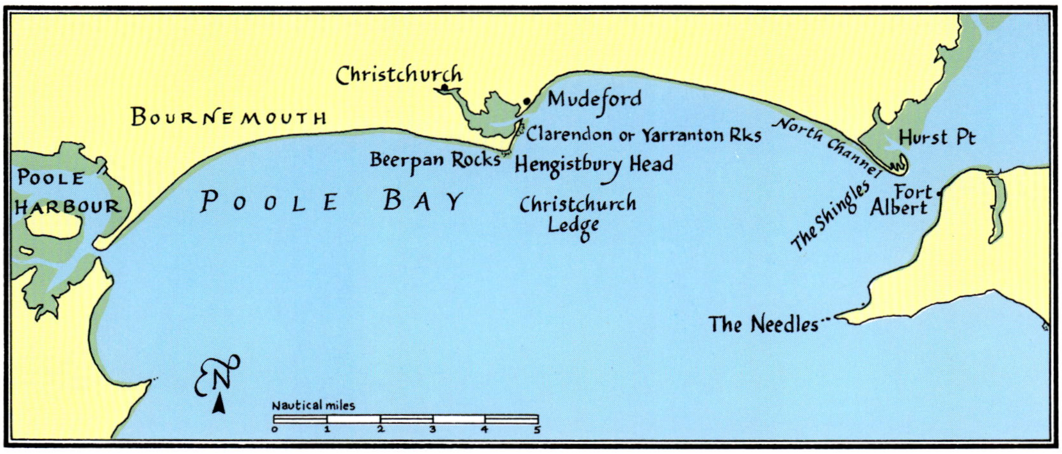

Right: Hengistbury Head and Christchurch from the south taken at LW. The Beerpan Rocks are clearly visible at the bottom left of the picture, as are the Clarendon (Yarranton) Rocks to the south of the entrance at the top right

to Christchurch Harbour lie the Clarendon or Yarranton Rocks, a ledge extending some 400m out from the centre of the sand spit.

The entrance to Christchurch Harbour is surrounded by sand bars, which may shift after gales, so great care should be taken and a careful eye kept on the depth sounder even in the buoyed channel. Tides in the entrance, the Run, are particularly fast on the ebb, reaching as much as 6 knots on springs. As a general rule, it is unsafe to attempt to enter Christchurch in onshore winds of Force 5 or more.

Christchurch Harbour is mainly shallow with few deep water channels and anchorages, and is therefore most popular with shoal draught yachts able to take the ground. The depth in the Run restricts entrance to yachts with less than about 1.6m draught, and once in the harbour the deepest water is towards the town of Christchurch. There are a few visitors' moorings at Christchurch Sailing Club.

East of Christchurch the Bay sweeps

Right: Christchurch entrance at HW. At the top is Hengistbury Head, where the rocky reefs of Beerpan Rocks and Clarendon Rocks can be seen at the top and centre left of the picture. The sand bars at the entrance often shift so a careful eye should be kept on the depth sounder when entering. On the ebb tides run very fast in the Run, the main channel into the harbour, and may reach 5 or 6 knots on springs. The entrance is, though, clearly buoyed. Mudeford is to the right

Left: Christchurch entrance at LW with The Run leading into the narrow entrance

Left: Hurst Narrows looking across the Shingles Bank. Even though some water is shown over the Shingles on charts in places, this information should not be trusted as the Bank has shifted considerably in recent years. Although this picture is indistinct, it shows the extent of the drying patches

Left: Christchurch Harbour from the north-west and looking towards the Needles in the distance

Below: Hurst Spit, Castle and Lighthouses looking across to Fort Albert on the Island. Behind Fort Albert the upper reaches of the River Yar can be seen. To the left is Mount Lake and the yachts on the right of the picture are using the North Channel

round past the low sandstone cliffs of Milford, Hordle and Barton on Sea towards the low Hurst shingle spit, guarding the entrance to the Solent and Keyhaven Lakes. A distinctive landmark here is the wave research platform one mile off the Milford shore and two miles to the west of the North Head buoy which marks the entrance of the North Channel.

The major hazard in the approaches to the Solent is the notorious Shingles Bank. With local knowledge there are short cuts to be taken across the Shingles, but they are not to be recommended as the bank shifts frequently, especially during southwesterly gales. In recent years, the Shingles have built up considerably and there are some parts which are barely awash at HW.

In the early years of this century the Shingles was a much more established feature, and there are those who claim to remember bushes growing on the bank. Today erosion is more of a problem, particularly of Hurst Spit, which is constantly being reinforced to prevent a breach.

The yachtsman approaching the Solent from the west has two choices, the deep water Needles Channel and the North Channel which runs close under Hurst beach and is entered via the North Head buoy. From Poole or Christchurch this is the more direct route and in heavy weather, when wind against tide conditions off the Bridge by the Needles causes dangerously breaking seas, it is the safer entrance. During the last War a French corvette was overturned in the seas off the Bridge. Some very confused seas may be experienced in the vicinity of Hurst, especially on the flood tide when the North Channel and Needles Channel streams meet, but these are rarely dangerous and may be avoided once past Hurst by taking a hike to the north-east. The alternative for boats entering the Solent and plugging the ebb is to stay close to the Island shore.

Chapter 3

Hurst to Calshot

After the narrows at Hurst the Solent opens up into a broad expanse of water. On the mainland side the marshy foreshore and mudflats between Keyhaven and Calshot shoal gently and, for the main part, evenly into deeper water. The tides are weaker close to the mainland shore and as a rule yachts stemming a foul tide can benefit by keeping within half a mile of the coast.

There are, however, a number of hazards to be avoided. From the west these are the Trap off Hurst; shoal water and Pennington Spit to the north of Hurst; the sewer outfall at Pennington; Lymington Spit, which extends about 100m south and 400m south-east of the Starting Platform at the east side of the entrance to Lymington River; Lepe Bank to the west of the entrance of Beaulieu River; the spit off Stansore Point to the east of Beaulieu with dolphins at its southern edge, and Calshot Spit itself.

Facing page: Hurst Point with Keyhaven Lake in the background. There is a good anchorage off the beach to the east of Hurst and room for a few yachts to anchor where the three boats are in the centre of the picture

Above: Hurst Point with the Trap clearly showing at the lower left of the picture. This hook-shaped shoal is open to the west and 'traps' many unwary yachts hugging the shore on the ebb to take advantage of the counter eddy there

Keyhaven

There is an excellent anchorage immediately inside Hurst Point which offers good shelter except from the north-east through to the south. Much of Keyhaven Lake dries at LW and there is only room for a few yachts to anchor just inside the entrance unless they are prepared to take the ground. At HW it is

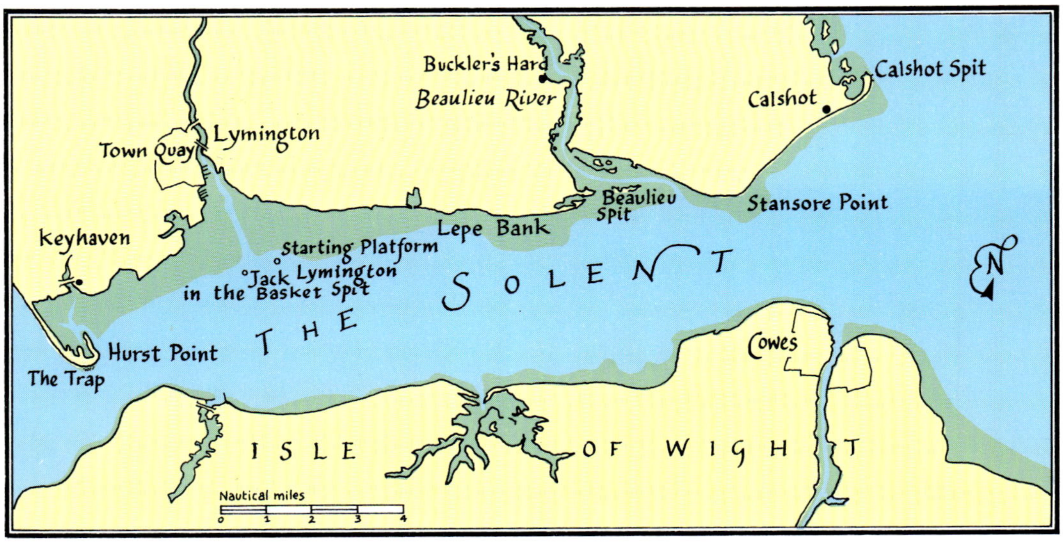

Right: Lymington Marina and ferry terminal

Below: Lymington River with the Yacht Haven in the centre and Lymington Marina and ferry terminal above. The ferries are a little disconcerting at first and should be given plenty of room as they manoeuvre in the river

Above: Keyhaven village and quay

possible for deep draught yachts to reach the quay, though there are few facilities here to attract the visiting yachtsman. However, there is great scope for exploration by dinghy in Mount, Keyhaven and Hawkers Lakes from either the Hurst or Keyhaven anchorages, and a visit to Hurst Castle and walk along the Spit is well worth the effort.

Lymington River

Lymington is one of the most attractive and popular of the Solent harbours. Apart from the two large marinas, Lymington Yacht Haven and Lymington Marina (Berthon), both of which have visitors' berths, Lymington Town Quay has alongside berths and mooring buoys though, like so many parts of the Solent, the Quay gets very crowded in summer months.

The entrance to the Lymington River is between the Jack in the Basket beacon and the Starting Platform. Although narrow in places, especially at LW, the river is clearly marked by posts and well lit. A regular ferry service runs between Lymington and Yarmouth on the Isle of Wight, and these ferries constitute the main hazard. Yachts and dinghies should keep well clear of them,

Right: Lymington Town Quay (centre). There are moorings for visiting yachts either alongside or on buoys opposite the quay, but it gets crowded in summer months. It is possible to dry out at the quay by prior arrangement with the Harbourmaster

Left: At LW there is precious little room for the ferry, seen here just off the Yacht Haven. Leading marks in the marina keep yachts clear of the shoals which lie to the south of the entrance

Above: Lymington River with the Lymington and Yacht Haven Marinas and the Island in the background. The Royal Lymington Yacht Club, which organises many major international events, is at the centre right of the picture, the ferry terminal at the bottom left

particularly in the narrow parts of the river, on corners, as the ferries 'drift' around them, and in strong cross-winds. There is often considerable wash from them and, as they push a fair volume of water ahead of them and conversely leave a 'hole' astern, it is not unusual for yachts in shallow water to find themselves temporarily aground in their wake as water returns to fill the 'vacuum' astern of the vessel.

As a major yachting centre, Lymington has almost every service the yachtsman might require and excellent shopping, restaurants and pubs.

Beaulieu River

Owned by Lord Montagu, the Beaulieu River is one of the least spoilt rivers on the South Coast. Winding inland for several miles, first inside the banks of Beaulieu Spit and then through gentle countryside, with the gardens of large houses sloping down to the water's edge, the main yachting centre on the river is at Buckler's Hard, site of the famous yard which built many of Nelson's ships. Most of the shipwrights' cottages remain today, including the master builder's house, now a popular pub, restaurant and hotel of the same name. There is a museum showing the history of Buckler's Hard and some houses are unchanged and furnished as set pieces.

The entrance of the Beaulieu River is shallow and there is little water over the bar at LW, especially springs. In general, deeper water is found just to the east of the leading marks on shore.

Both the entrance and the river are well marked, the former being lit. Until 1987, there was a shallow passage between Needs Ore Point and the mud flats known as the Bull Run, Needs Ore Channel or the Swashway, but this was closed owing to

Above: Lepe Bank is in the foreground, with Beaulieu Spit leading towards Stansore Point at the top of the picture

Below: Park Shore Banks lie to the west of Beaulieu Spit and Lepe Bank, seen here with the Beaulieu River in the background

Above: The spit at Stansore Point at LW springs, looking north-west towards the entrance to the Beaulieu River. Safe water at all states of the tide is found close up to the three posts at the lower left of the picture

Right: The lower reaches of Beaulieu River with Gin's Farm on the left

erosion and a bird sanctuary created.

Anchoring is permitted along the first reach of the river before it turns inland, otherwise visiting yachts may choose between the marina or pile moorings at Buckler's Hard or, by prior arrangement with the Harbourmaster, use one of the private moorings in the river. There is a yard and yacht chandler at Buckler's Hard, the Master Builder and a small general store, at which reasonable provisions and Off Licence facilities can be obtained.

Beaulieu River to Calshot

Immediately to the east of the entrance to the Beaulieu River are Stone and Stansore Points, with shoals extending up to 550m from Stansore. Yachts leaving the river and heading east should stand out into the Solent until the most southerly of the two beacons off Stansore Point bears approximately east (magnetic) and then pass outside them.

When turning the corner into Southampton Water there is adequate water for some distance to the west and north of NE Gurnard buoy, although Calshot Spit extends much closer to Bourne Gap buoy and the Calshot Spit catamaran light float, which marks the eastern end of the spit.

At HW there is adequate water over much of the spit, keeping to the east of the beacon marking the edge of the Calshot sewage outfall, but at LW it is advisable to keep close to but still outside the main channel, especially when there is shipping in the vicinity, when part of the channel is prohibited to yachtsmen (see Chapter 5 for

Above: The Marina at Buckler's Hard and the Agamemnon Boatyard, named after one of the warships built here

Below: The first reach of the Beaulieu River runs inside Beaulieu Spit, seen here exposed at LW. At the far left is Lepe Bank

Above: The river is navigable for several miles inland. Buckler's Hard Marina is on the right

full details). In particular, yachts heading up Southampton Water should avoid the temptation to make the short cut over apparently deep water between the red can Bourne Gap buoy and Black Jack, also a red can, just off Calshot Spit, as this leads directly over the shallowest part of the spit. Alternatively there is more water to the east of the main Thorn Channel, making sure to stay to the west of the small green West Knoll buoy which marks the northwestern extremity of the Bramble Bank (see also Chapter 5).

Right: Calshot Spit at the north-west corner of Southampton Water. Although Calshot can be crossed at HW, the tempting short cut it offers to yachts heading to or from the Hamble or Southampton is not worth the risk at other states of the tide

Chapter 4

Needles to Cowes

From the Bridge down the Needles Channel between a number of hazards on the island shore and the Shingles Bank, the main approaches to the western Solent meet up with the North Channel just short of Hurst Narrows. East of Hurst the channel widens out again past the popular and busy Isle of Wight harbours of Yarmouth, Newtown and the 'mecca' of yachting, Cowes.

Needles to Yarmouth

The familiar landmark of the Needles at the western extremity of the Isle of Wight marks the grave of many ships. The most notorious of these is the SS *Varvassi*, wrecked here in 1947, which has since come into contact with the keels of many yachts passing too close to the Needles. Although most of the wreck has broken up, there still remain three or four pieces, the largest being her boiler, and two of which dry at LW springs and lie about 100m from the lighthouse. Just to the north of the Needles is Goose Rock, and although there is a passage of deep water between this and the wreck it is not recommended. To the north-east of Goose Rock lies another historic wreck and the area surrounding it is prohibited, so in all this is

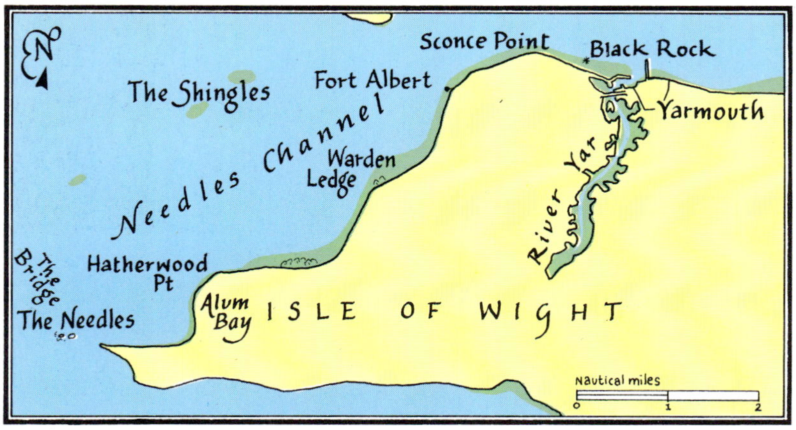

Left and right: The Needles now and then. On 5th January, 1947 the SS *Varvassi* was wrecked on the Needles. Today parts of the wreck are still a hazard and can clearly be seen here about 100m off the light at the centre right of the picture. Goose Rock is close by the light. To stay in deep water when rounding the Needles, keep the top of the lighthouse below the level of the cliffs above. There is a clear passage between the inner part of the wreck and Goose Rock but, as it is extremely difficult to judge distances at sea level and see any evidence of the wreck, it is not recommended

an area best given a wide berth.

With wind against tide, especially on the spring ebb, seas over the Bridge between the Needles and the west cardinal Bridge buoy become very confused and break heavily, and in these conditions it is often safer to leave or enter the Solent via the North Channel described in Chapter 2.

The Needles Channel, well marked and lit, leads between the Island and the Shingles Bank and there are no dangers on the Island side provided yachts keep close by the main channel. There are a number of rocks in Alum Bay and about two cables to the south-

Above: Alum Bay, with its distinctive multi-coloured cliffs, provides a sheltered anchorage with the wind between south and north-east

Right: Warden Ledge (foreground) extends ¼ mile out from Warden Point, its western extremity marked by the green Warden buoy. In the background are Hatherwood Point and the Needles

west of Hatherwood Point is the Five Fingers Rock. Between here and Fort Albert the main hazard is Warden Ledge which extends ¼ mile to the north-west of Warden Point. Further to the north-east is How Reef, but this does not extend as far offshore as Warden. Apart from reefs close to Fort Albert and the Round Tower, the coast can be followed closely to Sconce Point.

Yachts approaching or leaving the Solent via the Needles Channel and Hurst Narrows should keep a good look-out for shipping, especially astern for overtaking vessels and maintain a steady course. Although not as busy as the Eastern Solent in terms of commercial traffic, ships using this channel are not required to have pilots aboard and may be less used to the unpredicatable behaviour of some yachts than local masters and pilots.

Between Sconce and Yarmouth lies Black Rock, a dark volcanic outcrop in stark contrast with the surrounding sandy bottom, that dries at LW springs. The rock lies approximately half-way between the Black

Below: The rocky reefs between Fort Albert and Sconce Point (centre left) show well in this picture with the busy Solent beyond. The exceptional visibility when this picture was taken gives a clear view of the western Solent, to Yarmouth, Newtown and Egypt Point. In the very far distance, the white cliffs of Portsdown Hill above Portsmouth can be seen

Above: For visiting yachts Yarmouth is one of the Solent's most popular destinations, and it is not unusual for yachts to have to anchor or moor off in Yarmouth Roads

Left: Both Black Rock and the shoal patch some 50m to the north-west of the entrance to Yarmouth show well here. Black Rock lies about half-way between the Black Rock buoy and the shore

Rock buoy and the shore, with deep water between. Inshore of the rock is a shallow passage. In wind against tide conditions, close to Black Rock buoy a localised race, Fiddler's Race, can develop in fresh winds.

Yarmouth

At LW yachts coming from the west should not steer direct for the western end of the breakwater, as there is a shoal patch some 50m to the north-west. Otherwise the entrance is deep and the only hazards to avoid are the Lymington to Yarmouth ferries.

Yarmouth is almost completely given over to pile berths for visiting yachts, and is probably the most popular weekend harbour for Solent sailors. Most of the local boats moor above the new opening bridge. It is possible to lie alongside the quay for short periods, though for overnight stays the Harbourmaster will normally direct yachts to suitable piles. Yarmouth does get very crowded in summer months and it is not uncommon for the harbour to be closed at peak times as it is full and for yachts to have to anchor or moor outside.

Ashore are a number of pubs and restaurants but Yarmouth is a quiet town with few shops, though there is a chandler and boatyard. Seafood aficionados should not miss the Puffin fishery – cross the bridge and take the first track off to the left.

Above: The new swing bridge at Yarmouth, open here, was completed during 1988 and many local boats moor above the bridge in preference to the busy outer harbour. A dinghy trip up the River Yar (top right) is well worth the effort

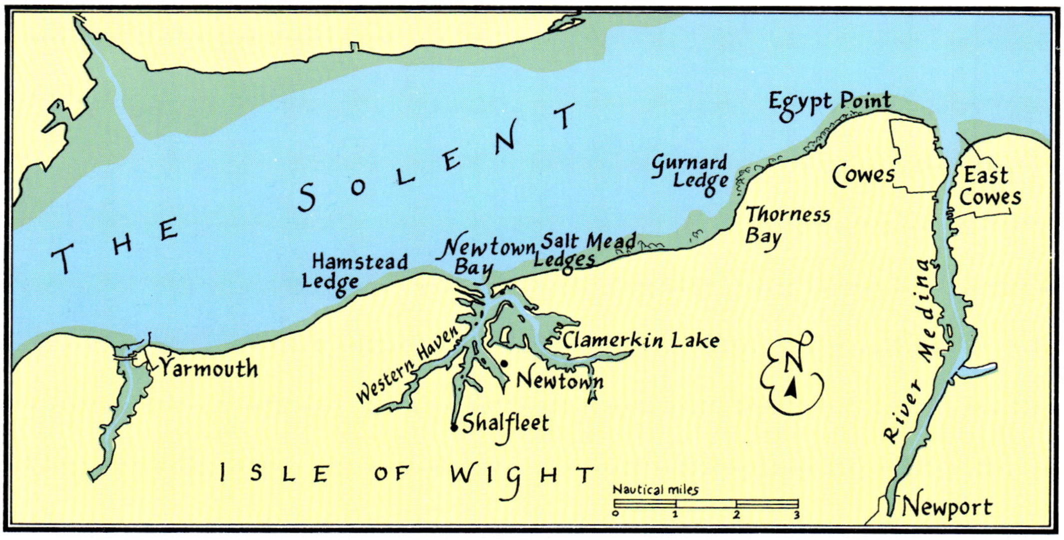

Above: dawn departure from the Newtown River

Right: Hamstead Ledge consists of a number of rocky spits that extend well beyond the end of the barrier. In good weather there is a clear passage about 200m inside the Hamstead Ledge buoy, which marks the deeper extremities of the ledge. The entrance to the Newtown River is at the top right of the picture

Left: Newtown at LW. Clamerkin Lake anchorage is in the foreground, with Newtown River leading off towards Shalfleet at the top left. The two small drying patches just inside the entrance are marked by withies and care should be taken not to cut the corner

Above: Although narrow the entrance to the Newtown River is deep with the shallowest water close by the small red spherical buoy in the approaches. Clamerkin Lake leads off the the left of the entrance and is a popular anchorage. There are a number of visitors' buoys in Shalfleet Creek and plenty of scope for shoal draught yachts able to take the ground

Newtown

Between Yarmouth and Newtown the only dangers are close inshore, with the exception of a number of large MoD mooring buoys to the south and east of Yarmouth and Hamstead Ledge. At its outer end this is marked by a green conical lighted buoy, but as the ledge is deep here it is safe to pass inside by about 200m in good weather. Further inshore, though, two shallow rocky ledges project offshore beyond the end of the barrier and there are further ledges to the west of the barrier, therefore the temptation to creep close to the end of the barrier out of the main tide

Above and right:
Newtown at HW and LW. At HW it is possible to travel by dinghy as far as and beyond Shalfleet Quay or explore the Western Haven. There are several visitors' moorings in the main part of the river (centre) and an anchorage in Clamerkin Lake (top right)

should be resisted at all times.

Shoal banks extend some way out from both sides of the entrance to the Newtown River, so on entry it is important first to locate the small red spherical buoy about 600m off and then enter on the leading marks on the eastern side, leaving the buoy to port by about 200m. Once inside the river divides, the left-hand leading to the anchorage in Clamerkin Lake, the right towards a number of visitors' moorings and Shalfleet Quay. This branch divides again with the drying Western Haven offering plenty of scope for dinghy exploration. Early morning provisions, bread, milk, and water in butts are available at Lower Hamstead Farm.

The Newtown River, administered by the National Trust, is one of the most delightful of all South Coast harbours and so, like Yarmouth, is often full at weekends, with many yachts anchoring outside to the west of the entrance. There is nothing except the river, the wildlife – and other yachts. A visit to the New Inn, landing at Shalfleet Quay and walking the mile or so to the pub, is worthwhile provided you get your tides

Below: The extensive shingle shoals to the eastern side of the entrance to the Newtown River have a spherical red buoy marking their extremity. On entering the river, leave this about 200m to port before picking up the leading marks. There is a green spherical buoy marking the bank on the western sides of the entrance. Hamstead Ledge can be seen at the top right of the picture

Left: Saltmead Ledges lie just under a mile to the east of Newtown, which can be seen at the top right of the picture. There is, however, deep water for 300m inside the Saltmead Ledges buoy

right and don't linger too long over your pint. Shalfleet Creek dries by the Quay and it's a long dinghy push through the mud back to deep water.

Newtown to Cowes

Immediately to the east of the entrance of Newtown is a shingle bank extending some way out towards deep water and beyond that a number of shoals towards Saltmead Ledges, just under a mile to the east. The outer extremity of the Ledges is marked by the Saltmead green conical lighted buoy, and it is possible to pass close inside this. Beyond Saltmead is Thorness Bay where there are two reefs, Quarry Ledge and a line of rocks that extend out from the middle of the bay. Both of these can be avoided by sailing along the 10m contour using a depth sounder, as the sea-bed is steeply shelving here and so it may be clearly identified. This is also a good ploy in poor visibility because

Right: There is a reef in the centre of Thorness Bay with an unmarked isolated outcrop approximately 100m to seaward and 600m from the shore

Left: Gurnard Ledge is shown clearly here by the breaking wake of a passing vessel. One of the more notorious of the Solent's hazards, it extends in a curve to the north-east out from Gurnard Head for a distance of ½ mile. Quarry Ledge and Thorness Bay are at the top right of the picture

the same contour will allow Gurnard Ledge to be passed safely and lead around Egypt Point and into Cowes Roads, though a good look-out should be kept for a line of mooring buoys to the ENE of the Point.

Gurnard Ledge is one of the Solent's most notorious hazards, mainly because the tide runs fast between Gurnard Head and Egypt Point and it is tempting to hug the shore to avoid the worst of the foul stream. The rocky ledge extends out some distance and is steep-to, so there will be little warning from the depth sounder. The safe strategy along this length of coast is to stay on the rhumb line between Saltmead and Gurnard Ledge buoys, even if it means stemming a foul tide for a few more minutes.

Egypt Point itself can be passed close-to, well inside the Gurnard north cardinal buoy, though there are rocky outcrops towards its eastern end. Avoid the temptation to cut the corner immediately to

Right: Egypt Point looking west down the Solent. A rocky reef extends just over 100m out from the Point just to the west of the light

Right: Cowes and the Medina River. Ancasta Marina is in the centre right of the picture, with the Cowes Marina at East Cowes beyond. In the background can be seen the pile and pontoon moorings at the Folly. The boats in the centre of the picture are on private small craft moorings

the west of the Royal Yacht Squadron (easily identified by its red and white striped canopy) as there is a rocky ledge extending to the east, with its outer end half-way between the Squadron and the green No 3 buoy. To be sure leave this buoy to starboard when entering Cowes. Beware of the strong tidal set across the entrance.

Cowes

Cowes is still considered as the mecca of yachting and every other year hosts the world's most prestigious offshore racing event, the Admiral's Cup, as well as Cowes Week, the UK's largest annual regatta, usually run over the first week in August.

The Medina River divides Cowes and, for the moment at any rate, it is West Cowes that is the major yachting centre. There are, however, plans to develop East Cowes with a new marina and breakwater, much needed as Cowes is very exposed to winds with any north in them when even the Ancasta Marina (ex-Groves & Gutteridge) can become very uncomfortable.

The main channel is clearly marked through Cowes and up the River Medina as far as the Folly Inn, although there is a shoal patch in the centre of the channel 200m past the chain ferry and parts of the river in the approaches to the Folly moorings are shallow. Otherwise, yachts should keep an eye out for the hydrofoil in the harbour entrance and steer clear of the Red Funnel ferries when they are manoeuvring between the West and East Cowes terminals.

For the visitor there are any number of choices. There are a several visitors' mooring buoys to the south of the Squadron off the Parade on the seafront; Ancasta Marina has a good number of visitors' berths, but these are expensive even if they do have the advantage of being close to the centre of the town; just to the south of the marina there are pontoons on piles and a limited number

Above: Looking out over the Solent from Cowes to Calshot and Southampton Water. Cowes Marina just shows through the mist at the bottom of the picture

Right: The Folly Inn, a popular watering hole for visiting yachtsmen and locals alike

of alongside pontoon berths whilst further upstream, past the chain ferry, there are more pile moorings, clearly marked for visitors. The Cowes Marina at East Cowes has visitors' berths and there are more pontoon/pile moorings on the right-hand side of the river close to the Folly Inn, a popular watering hole.

Further upstream on the eastern side of the Medina River is the locked Medina Yacht Harbour, accessible approximately three hours either side of HW and it is also possible to carry the tide right up to Newport, where there are pontoons for yachts able to take the ground.

Cowes has all amenities for yachtsmen from chandlers to yards and a good selection of shops, restaurants and pubs.

Above: The Medina Yacht Harbour

Below: It is possible to carry the tide as far as Newport, where there are pontoons for yachts able to dry out at LW

Chapter 5

Southampton Water and the East Solent

Southampton Water, fed by the Rivers Itchen, Test and, to a lesser extent, Hamble, leads many miles inland and gives access to the major deep-water port of Southampton. Although Southampton has lost the glory of the days of the great ocean liners it is still a busy port, and with the additional traffic going to and from the Fawley oil refinery a considerable volume of shipping uses this waterway.

Shipping and hazards

Yachtsmen should at all times remember that shipping has right of way in Southampton Water and its approaches and take appropriate action, which should cause few problems as there is adequate water for small craft outside the main buoyed channel.

In particular, the Port of Southampton has instituted a 'no go area' for small craft when there is any shipping in the area

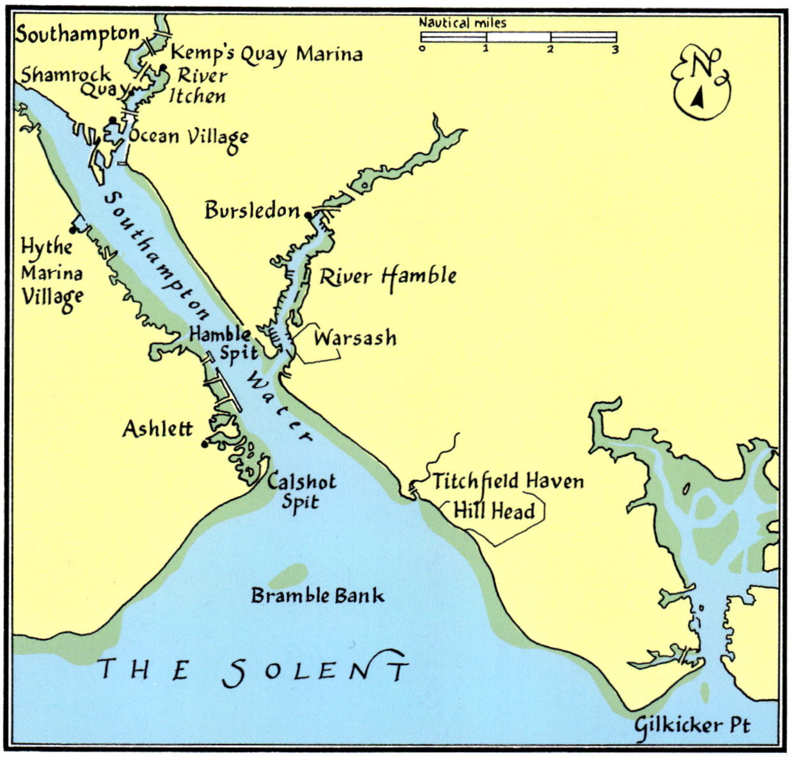

Right: Ashlett Creek at LW

Left: Ashlett Creek meanders through the mudflats on the western side of Southampton Water almost right below the chimneys of Fawley refinery. Drying to a mere trickle at LW, the entrance is just 200m from the southern end of the main jetty off Fawley. Ashlett Mill (centre left) is now used as a club by Esso

Above: posts in the entrance to the Hamble River clearly mark the southern edge of Hamble Spit, although this also extends some distance to the north. Hamble Point Marina is in the centre of the picture, with Port Hamble above and to the left. There are visitors' pile moorings off Hamble and Warsash (centre right)

bounded by Bourne Gap buoy, North Thorn buoy, Calshot Spit Light Float, Calshot buoy, Castle Point buoy and Reach buoy.

Leading off Southampton Water is the Hamble River, home to thousands of yachts and small craft. Off Netley are a number of moorings whilst the recently-developed Hythe Marina and Ocean Villages have increased the popularity of the area. There are also many yachts kept on the River Itchen at Shamrock Quay and Kemp's Quay Marina.

The main hazards in the approaches to Southampton Water are the Bramble Bank, a large shoal 1½ miles to the north of Cowes, its southeastern extremity marked by a distinctive radar reflector post, and Calshot Spit described in Chapter 3. Although well buoyed, strong cross-tides, particularly the east-going flood, can set the unwary down on to the bank, and yachts heading across the Solent from Southampton Water to Cowes should take particular care to stay to the west of the small green conical West

Above: Hamble Point Marina with Warsash on the opposite bank. The Harbourmaster's office is the round tower on the Warsash shore and the white building on the right is the Rising Sun, a popular yachtsman's pub

Left: the 'Bond Street' of British yachting, with Port Hamble Marina at centre left

Above: Mercury Yacht Harbour with Moody's Swanwick Marina at the top of the picture. Between Mercury and Moody's on the eastern shore are the Crableck pontoons and Universal Shipyard marina

Knoll buoy. At LW springs the bank partially dries and there is a tradition, started by the late Uffa Fox and continued sporadically, of a cricket match played on the bank at equinoctial springs.

On the western side of Southampton Water there are drying banks inside the line of the several jetties, and whilst there is water outside the buoyed big ship channel more is to be found on the eastern side with the exception of Hamble Spit and banks to the south-east of the entrance to Hamble River and to the north-west of Netley, where the drying shoals extend almost right to the edge of the buoyed channel. Both are clearly marked, with posts in the entrance to the River Hamble, though Hamble Spit extends some way to the north-west of these. Bald Head buoy is at the southeastern extremity

Left: the entrance to Hythe Marina Village on the western shore of Southampton Water, one of several recent South Coast marina village developments

Above: A. H. Moody & Sons is one of the longest-established yacht yards on the South Coast, and the Moody family still run the active boatbuilding business and operate Swanwick Marina. On the far left are the pontoons of the Elephant and Deacons boatyards, and just hidden from view on the near left is the Jolly Sailor pub, immortalised in TV's sailing soap, *Howard's Way*, in which the village of Tarrant is modelled on Bursledon just to the left of the picture. The A27 Swanwick Bridge is the limit for sailing yachts, though many powerboats are kept further inland below the M27

of the banks on the eastern side of the entrance. Between the Hamble and Gilkicker Point there are uneven drying banks close inshore and it is best to keep an offing of 600m or so. Just to the south-east of the small, drying Titchfield Haven is an area reserved for water-skiing and off Lee Point a shallow, buoyed sewage outfall with a wreck some 500m to seaward of this. At Titchfield Haven is the active Hill Head Sailing Club.

Hamble River

The River Hamble, sometimes known as the Bond Street of yachting, is home to thousands of yachts kept on piles in the river or in one of the marinas. One of the closest of South Coast harbours to London with excellent motorway links, Hamble is the most crowded and offers first-class services

Right: Shamrock Quay (centre right) was previously owned and operated by Camper & Nicholsons, and many of their great yachts were built and refitted here. The construction of the Itchen Bridge restricted the size of yacht that could pass underneath, and shortly after the yard was sold. There is still a specialist yacht builder, Southampton Marine Services, at Shamrock Quay. On the left-hand side of the picture is Kemp's Quay Marina, just below Northam Bridge

Left: Ocean Village has been developed from the old Princess Alexandra Dock on the River Itchen just below the Itchen Bridge. Shamrock Quay can be seen at the top left of the picture

Right: Titchfield Haven is a small, drying harbour close by Hill Head at the south eastern side of Southampton Water

to yachtsmen. There are visitors' berths in all the large marinas, though it is advisable to book in advance, and some visitors' pile moorings at Warsash and opposite near the Hamble shore. The upper reaches of the Hamble are now frequented by many tripper boats, as Bursledon is the mythical village of Tarrant in the television soap *Howard's Way* and the Elephant Boatyard Tom Howard's Mermaid yard.

Above: the Bramble Bank lies at the confluence of Southampton Water and the Solent, here looking north-west across from the Bramble Bank Post and the Fawley Power Station chimney

Top: Stokes Bay looking toward Gilkicker Point. The entrance to Portsmouth Harbour is at the top left

Ashlett, Hythe and the River Itchen

Opposite Hamble River is the small, drying Ashlett Creek, nestling right under the towering chimneys of Fawley Refinery where the Jolly Sailor pub is worth a HW visit. Further up Southampton Water and in the River Itchen are the recent marina village developments of Hythe Marina Village and Ocean Village. Just above the Itchen Bridge is Shamrock Quay and just before Northam Bridge Kemp's Quay.

Chapter 6

Cowes to Bembridge

Although well populated, there are only two harbours on the north east coast of the Isle of Wight suitable for yachts, Wootton and Bembridge, both of which dry to some extent at low water. The eastern Solent is, however, busy with commercial shipping as it offers deeper water access than the west. Apart from ferries between Portsmouth, Ryde and Fishbourne there is cross-Channel traffic from Portsmouth, large vessels plying to and from the Port of Southampton and the Fawley Refinery and Naval Ships out of Portsmouth.

Right: the Shrape Mud looking west towards Cowes. As this extends some way to the south of the breakwater, the temptation to cut the corner should be resisted

Above: Norris Rocks, just to the east of Cowes, are another hazard for anyone creeping inshore to cheat the tide. From seaward their position can be identified by a clearing in the trees (far left) leading down to the beach

Cowes to Wootton Creek

The Island coast between Cowes and Bembridge Ledge has a number of hazards and obstructions, the most notorious being Ryde Sands and Bembridge Ledge, of which the latter has played unwelcome host to several well-known racing yachts in recent years. Additionally, there are man-made obstructions such as large concrete blocks on the Peel Bank, the submerged barrier to the south of No Man's Land Fort and the shingle spit inshore of St Helen's Fort, though the buoyed channel approaching Bembridge cuts through this.

Between East Cowes and Castle Point is the Shrape Mud, which extends some

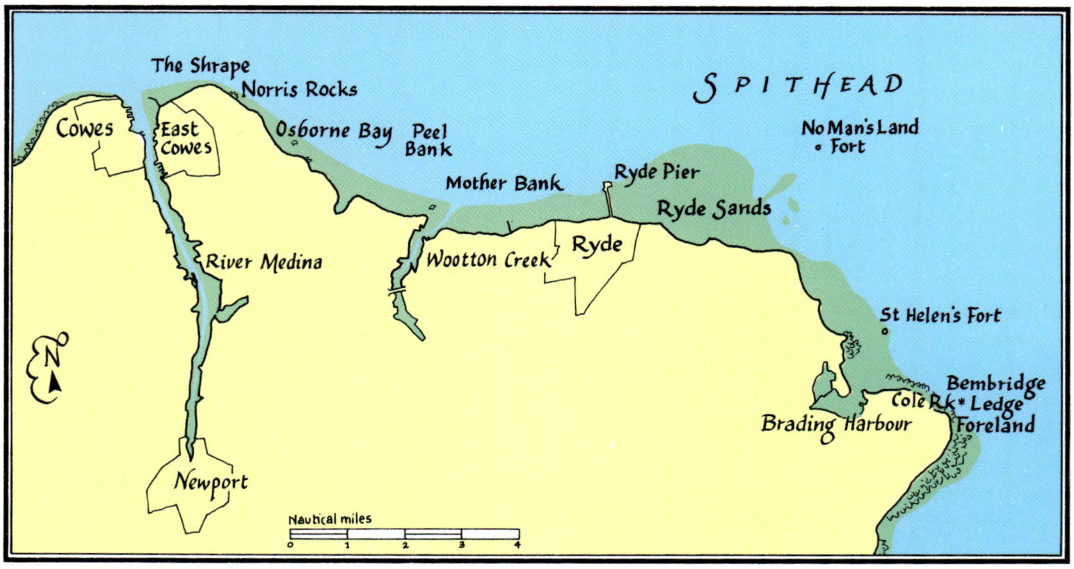

Left and above: Wootton Creek at HW and LW. The Creek dries almost completely at LW, except in the fairway which is dredged for the Portsmouth/Fishbourne ferries. The Royal Victoria Yacht Club is close by the ferry terminal on the eastern shore

distance to the north-east of the end of the breakwater, so the temptation to take a short cut should be resisted. As a further disincentive to cutting the corner, Old Castle Point Ledge and Norris Rocks at the western end of Osborne Bay will provide yet more obstacles to anyone creeping close inshore to cheat a foul tide. The Norris buoy may, however, be safely passed inside about half-way between the buoy and the shore. Osborne Bay is a popular anchorage in offshore winds, though it is shallow inshore with a number of rocky outcrops. Although the creek dries, it is worth anchoring off King's Quay at HW and exploring by dinghy.

Peel Bank buoy marks the northern extremity of Peel Bank and to the east is the Mother Bank buoy. Although Peel Bank is marked as being relatively flat, there are several obstructions, mainly large concrete blocks. One of these is marked by a wreck buoy off King's Quay and another to the south-east of Peel Bank buoy. There is also a water-skiing area off King's Quay.

Above: Wootton Rocks lie to the west of the entrance of the drying Wootton Creek. The large posts at the centre right are the ferry terminal

Below: No Man's Land Fort looking south-west, with Ryde Sands to the right and the sand spit which leads out towards the fort on the left

Wootton Creek

Immediately to the west of the entrance of Wootton Creek and to the north-east of Wootton Point are the Wootton Rocks, and so yachts approaching from the west should not work too close inshore, instead they

should aim a little to the north of Wootton beacon.

Although there is a dredged deep-water channel in the approaches to Wootton Creek for the Portsmouth/Fishbourne ferries, most of the Creek now dries at LW, and even the pool is virtually dry at LW springs. Shoal draught yachts can lie to piles or on one of the visitors' moorings, but it is forbidden to anchor in the fairway or by the hard near the ferry terminal. In offshore winds there is an anchorage to the west of Wootton Beacon. Ashore the hospitable Royal Victoria Yacht Club welcomes visiting yachtsmen.

Wootton to Bembridge

To the east of Ryde Pier lies the great swathe of Ryde Sands, covered at HW and marked at its northern edge by the SW Mining Ground buoy and the conspicuous Sandhead Pile post, though this is inshore of the edge of the bank. As can be seen in the photograph, Ryde Sand is U-shaped, open to the east, and so a yacht working west in apparently deep water may suddenly find herself aground with the only exit being the way she came in. On an ebb tide this could lead to a long and embarrassing wait, although give plenty of time to inspect the

Above: Ryde Sands extend well out beyond the end of Ryde Pier and are shaped in a rough U open to the east. No Man's Land Fort is at the top left with a ferry leaving the Solent just beyond, and in the sun's reflection can be seen the sand spit leading out towards the Fort

Above and top: St Helen's Fort and the approaches to Bembridge at HW and LW. The buoyed channel is to the right – as can be seen in the LW photograph

Right: Bembridge Harbour at HW and LW. The marina at the bottom right of the HW picture has some visitors' moorings, though there is little depth here at LW. The position of deepest water in the approach channel can be seen in the LW picture

anti-fouling and explore the possibilities of Ryde Sands for the bucket and spade brigade. The annual Round the Island Race gives shoreside spectators plenty of entertainment as yachts attempt to work too close inshore to avoid the foul flood tide. As a general rule, a course just outside the direct line between SW Mining Ground and No Man's Land Fort will take a yacht clear of all dangers here.

Inshore of No Man's Land Fort a long sand spit extends out from the shore and between this and the fort itself there is a submerged barrier and, although it may be tempting to cross this at HW, great care should be taken as the stumps of the original barrier protrude from the sea-bed.

A direct course from No Man's Land Fort to St Helen's Fort off Bembridge will, near HW, take yachts clear of the hazards in Seaview, Seagrove and Priory Bays, but at LW it is best to keep a little further offshore.

The entrance to Bembridge is inside St Helen's Fort and is clearly marked. However, like most of Bembridge, this virtually dries at LW, although in June 1989 dredging operations were under way to create an approach with 2m depth at MLWS to allow yachts with up to 6ft draught to leave or enter at all stages of the tide. The approach beacon has a tide gauge which indicates depth at the shallowest part of the approach channel. There are some visitors' moorings in the marina by the Brading Haven YC but even here there is little depth at LW, though as the mud is soft deep-keeled yachts can take the ground safely here. There are plans for a £10 million redevelopment of Bembridge Harbour.

As with the western extremity of the Isle of Wight, so the easternmost point is marked by dangerous rocky reef, Bembridge Ledge, and an accompanying wreck a little way off. In recent years, several prominent racing yachts have come to grief on both the wreck and the Ledge when taking short cuts well inside the Bembridge Ledge buoy.

The Ledge extends out from Whitecliff Bay, with the most eastern Sharpus Rocks some 500m off the Foreland. The wreck of the *Empress Queen*, a paddle steamer which was wrecked here in 1916, lie some distance out from these (see picture). To the north and the north-east of the Sharpus Rocks,

Right: Bembridge Ledge looking north-west towards the entrance to Portsmouth Harbour. Just above the tip of the ledge, Sharpus Rocks, can be seen Dicky Dawe Rocks

about 600m from the Foreland, are Dicky Dawe and Cole Rocks and, although neither dries, they are hazardous enough to steer well clear of. It is possible to take a short cut a little inside the Bembridge Ledge buoy but, unless familiar with these waters, it is probably a temptation best avoided.

Above: The appropriately-named Sharpus Rocks, the easternmost drying extremity of Bembridge Ledge, are at the centre left of the picture, with Long Ledge, Whitecliff Bay and Culver Cliffs beyond. At the far left of the picture the remains of the wreck of the *Empress Queen* can be seen (arrowed). In the distance is Sandown Bay, Shanklin and Dunnose

Left: Bembridge Ledge, looking deceptively deep, at HW with the Ledge buoy in the foreground

Chapter 7

Portsmouth and Langstone Harbours

Increased demand for South Coast moorings in recent years has led to both Portsmouth and Langstone Harbours becoming more popular amongst yachtsmen. Whilst neither is as attractive as their near neighbour, Chichester Harbour, both are well-placed for access to the eastern Solent harbours. Although both harbours are large, they dry out extensively, but there are a number of deep water channels where many small craft are moored and new marina developments in both harbours.

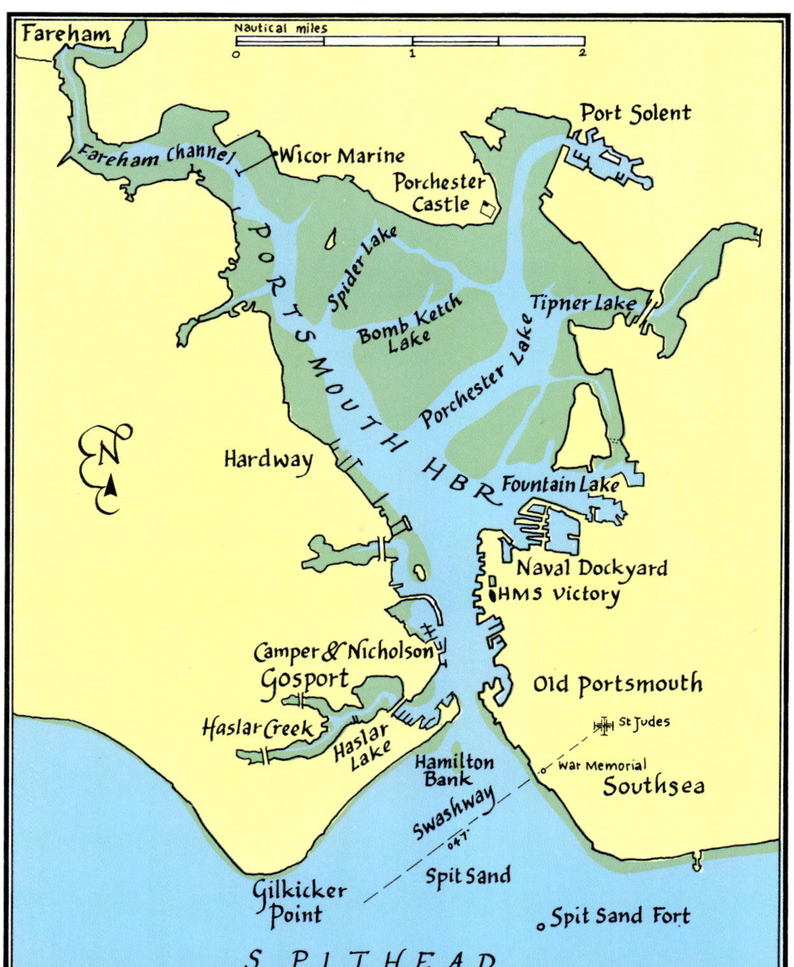

Portsmouth Harbour

Portsmouth Harbour is both an important Naval base and an active ferry port, with services to the Isle of Wight and to France. The narrow entrance can become very busy and there is a small boat channel on the western side, which yachts of less than 20m in length are required to use and may only do so under power if fitted with engines. Boats entering the harbour may also do so close by the eastern shore, but this is prohibited when leaving. At all times

Right: Haslar Lake is in the foreground with the Joint Services pontoons at the extreme left. Blockhouse Fort is at the western side of the entrance with the Small Boat Channel close by. There is one of the Gosport ferries alongside the jetty just below Camper & Nicholsons, and at the top centre of the picture are the moorings off the Hardway Sailing Club with Fareham Lake extending right into the distance

Top right: Looking north-west into Portsmouth Harbour along the main channel. Small craft of less than 20m are required to use the Small Boat Channel on the western side of the entrance and observe the entry signals shown on the Blockhouse signal station. The War Memorial on the sea front (lower right the picture) is the front transit marking the Swashway between Hamilton and Spit Banks. Immediately above the entrance is Camper & Nicholsons Marina

Left: Whale Island, the ferry terminal in Fountain Lake and Naval Dockyard looking south-west across towards the entrance of Portsmouth Harbour

Left: Portsmouth Harbour at LW. Camper & Nicholsons Marina and Cold Harbour are in the foreground, with Weevil Lake to the left and above and Hardway at the extreme left of the picture. The Naval Dockyard is opposite Campers on the right. Behind the smoke, Fountain Lake leads off towards the ferry terminals. Portchester Lake branches off to the right in the centre of the picture and just below the white cliffs of Portsdown Hill are the red roofs of Port Solent

Above and left: Fareham, Spider and Bomb Ketch Lakes at HW and LW looking towards the north-east. Fareham Lake leads off to the left, Spider lake is in the centre and Bomb Ketch Lake branches off the main channel to the right. Pewit Island is between Fareham and Spider Lakes in the colour picture

Right: Looking south-east across the harbour down Fareham Lake at LW. The Wicor Marine Pier is at the centre left of the picture

yachtsmen should keep a good look-out for ships manoeuvring and keep well clear. When large vessels are entering or leaving the harbour, entry to small craft may be prohibited and appropriate signals are shown from the Blockhouse signal station on the western side of the entrance. At springs the tide may run at up to 5 knots.

The main channel approaching Portsmouth runs between the Southsea shore and to the east of Spit Sand Fort. However, yachts approaching from the west may use the Swashway between Hamilton Bank and Spit sand using onshore transits. From the east there is a submerged barrier running nearly two miles from Eastney to Horse Sand Fort, but there are two passages through this offering a short cut for yachts coming from Chichester or Langstone. The inner Boat Passage should not be attempted by deep draught yachts near LW, though there is marginally greater depth at the second passage, marked by a dolphin about 3/4 mile off Southsea Beach.

Immediately inside the harbour Haslar Lake, with moorings and pontoons almost exclusively used by Service-owned craft, opens up on the left. The Joint Services

Below: Heavy Reach and Fareham Lake leading towards the town of Fareham. Electricity cables span the Lake (centre left) giving 16m clearance at MHWS

Right:: Portchester Lake at LW (centre left) branching off the main part of the harbour, with a ferry leaving the terminal in Fountain Lake at the far right. Hardway is at the bottom left

Left: Portchester Castle with the new Port Solent and Oyster Quay developments beyond. Portchester Lake has now been dredged to allow access to Port Solent at all states of tide

Sailing Club operates from here and has a number of pontoon berths close to Haslar Bridge. HMS *Victory* and HMS *Warrior* are on the eastern shore, with the Camper & Nicholsons yard and marina opposite. The busy green and white Gosport ferries shuttle across between the station on the eastern shore and a jetty just south of Camper & Nicholsons yard and marina.

Further into the harbour the Naval Dockyard is on the right-hand side, with the ferry terminals just beyond in Fountain Lake. Beyond this the main channel splits, with Portchester Lake branching off to the right and the Fareham Channel continuing past the active Hardway Sailing Club. Beyond this two more channels, Bomb Ketch and Spider Lakes, are off to the right before the Fareham Channel continues with deep water to just beyond the Wicor Marine pier on the right-hand side. Although there is little depth at Fareham at LW, the mud is soft enough for deep-keeled yachts to remain upright.

Portchester Lake is deep as far as Tipner Lake and there is a marked and recently dredged channel right up to the newly developed Port Solent marina village, beyond Portchester Castle.

There are few areas in Portsmouth where yachts can anchor and most visitors' berths are to be found at Camper & Nicholsons, Hardway or Wicor Marine.

Right: Port Solent looking north-east, with the M27 beyond. The channel leading to Port Solent has been dredged to allow access at all states of the tide

Above: The small boat channel through the submerged barrier off Eastney is marked by a dolphin some ¾ mile from the beach

Right: Approaches and entrance to Langstone Harbour, with the East Winner to the right and the Fairway buoy in the centre of the picture

Left: The East and West Winners at the entrance to Langstone Harbour show dramatically in this picture, looking south-east

Left: Langstone Harbour at HW. Eastney Point is on the western side of the entrance, and to the left of this Eastney Lake and at the far left Langstone Marina. Sinah Lake branches off to the right just past the right-hand side of the entrance

Langstone Harbour

Langstone is one of the least developed of South Coast harbours and yet offers a less hazardous entrance than Chichester, and although, like Portsmouth, much of the harbour dries, there is plenty of water in the main channels even at LW.

To the west of the entrance are the West Winner sands and entrance from this direction, keeping to seaward of a clearly marked wreck beacon, is made from the Langstone Fairway buoy. The more extensive East Winner sands mean that yachts coming from Chichester Harbour need to take a dog leg out to the south cardinal East Winner buoy to be safely clear of this and the Hayling Shoal. Once at the Langstone Fairway buoy entry is straightforward, making allowance for cross-streams. Tides may run at up to 5 knots on the ebb and, like Chichester, the entrance should be avoided in strong onshore winds when the ebb is running.

Once inside the harbour, immediately to the left is Eastney Lake which has a dredged channel leading to Langstone Marina which is tidal with a sill at its entrance. To the right,

Right: Langstone at LW looking south-east. The extent of the West Winner is clearly seen, and at the centre left of the picture, just below Sinah Lake, is the dark wreck of one of the huge concrete Mulberry pontoons built here during the last War in preparation for the Normandy invasion. Eastney Lake is just inside the western side of the entrance and at the far right, Langstone Marina

Left: Sinah Lake and the Langstone Channel at LW looking towards the town of Havant

Left: The main channel divides into the Broom Channel (centre right) and the deeper Langstone Channel, seen leading off to the left of the picture. The main anchorage is in the Langstone Channel

Sinah Lake leads off about 200m short of the distinctive wreck of one of the huge concrete pontoons, some of which were made in Langstone during the last War and towed across to the Normandy beaches to create the artificial Mulberry Harbour at Arromanches for D-day landings.

Further into the harbour the channel divides into the Broom and Langstone Channels, the latter leading up to Havant Quay and towards Langstone Bridge and Chichester Harbour.

Although Langstone Harbour has few facilities, there are some visitors' moorings on the east side of the entrance and a deep-water anchorage in Langstone Channel. At the time of writing the future of Langstone Marina was uncertain, as plans to develop it into a marina village were causing much local controversy. In the meantime, it lies empty until the dispute is settled, but up-to-date information for those wishing to visit Langstone can be obtained by 'phoning the Harbour Office (0705 463419) or by calling on VHF Channel 16 (working Channel 12) shortly before arrival.

Right and below: Langstone Bridge between the mainland and Hayling Island at HW and LW, with the reaches of Chichester Harbour beyond

Right: Langstone Marina, virtually empty in 1989, lies just inside the western side of the entrance

Chapter 8

Chichester Harbour

Although smaller than Poole, Chichester Harbour boasts considerably more variety and a greater proportion is navigable at LW. There are four main channels, Emsworth, Chichester, Thorney and Bosham, and on the shores of the harbour are the villages of Itchenor and Bosham and the town of Emsworth, whilst close by to the east is the city of Chichester.

There are numerous drying and deep-water moorings and five marinas, of which only two, Sparkes Yacht Harbour and Northney, are accessible at all states of the tide, though the latter only has enough water in the approaches for shoal draught yachts at LW.

Chichester Harbour and approaches

Chichester has a great deal to offer. For day sailing there is a wide variety of choice in its sheltered waters, especially for shoal draught yachts and those able to take the ground, there are several active sailing and yacht clubs and a great deal of dinghy racing takes place. With the backdrop of the Sussex Downs a few miles inland and many miles of navigable waterways, it is deservedly one of the most popular South Coast harbours.

For many years the harbour has been administered by the Chichester Harbour Conservancy, which has prevented commercial exploitation and preserved much of the harbour in its natural state for recreation and wildlife preservation. Apart from fishing boats, there is no commercial

Above: The main deep water channel in the entrance runs close to the Hayling shore. Hayling Island Sailing Club is on Sandy Point at the centre left with Mengham Rythe leading off just beyond it towards Sparkes Yacht Harbour. Beyond is Mill Rythe and the main Emsworth Channel

Far left: Chichester Bar Beacon, taken near low water. The extent of the shoals of the West Pole Sands to the south west of the beacon is clearly shown by the breaking seas. The picture shows Eastoke Point at the top left and The Winner at the top right

Left: The East Pole Sands with the two Targets clearly showing

Right: East Pole Sands looking west towards Langstone Harbour and the Solent. The Bar Beacon can be seen at the top left

Below: Sparkes Yacht Harbour with Sandy Point and Hayling Island Sailing Club behind

Above: Emsworth Channel looking south with Sweare Deep branching off at the centre right of the picture.

traffic. The Conservancy has greater powers than most harbour authorities, and yachts are expected to stick to the letter of the Collision Regulations over such matters as the correct use of lights and shapes when anchoring or motor-sailing. There is an overall speed limit of 6 knots.

The entrance and approaches to Chichester Harbour are, in most conditions, straightforward and safe, but entry for deeper yachts is best left until half tide. Entry on the ebb may be difficult as tides run at speeds over 5 knots at springs. However, in fresh onshore winds, particularly if against the ebb tide, it has a well deserved reputation on account of its depth, the extensive bars and shoals and the huge wind over tide seas that can build up, and it should be avoided in heavy weather. A number of yachts have, over the years, been lost here.

To the west of the entrance the West Pole Sands extend some ¾ mile south from Eastoke Point. Since the Bar Beacon was established, these have moved further some way to the south-west, as can be seen in the accompanying photograph. Visiting yachts should avoid the temptation to steer for the beacon and stay well off until the entry marks can be identified.

East Pole Sands stretch as much as one mile from the West Wittering beach, and near LW it is advisable for yachts coming from the east to steer for a point a mile or so south of the Bar Beacon before making their approach.

Once over the bar, the entrance itself, close under the Hayling shore, is deep, with the Winner sands to the east. Past the distinctive Hayling Island Sailing Club buildings on Sandy Point the channel divides into three, with Mengham Rythe leading off to the west, Chichester Channel to the east and the Emsworth Channel due north.

Emsworth Channel

The main part of Mengham Rythe dries, although there are some deep pools. Off

Left: Emsworth, the Yacht Harbour (left centre), Mill and Mill Pond. The water at the top left is the Thorney Channel

Mengham is Sparkes Yacht Harbour and the entrance to this is dredged. The Yacht Harbour has 140 permanent and twenty visitors' berths and, as it is close to the entrance, is convenient for anyone making an overnight stop on passage.

Like Mengham, Mill Rythe, just under a mile to the north, leads off to the west and has enough water for yachts to stay afloat at LW, though there is a drying patch at its entrance. It is possible to anchor here clear of the moorings, as it is anywhere in the Emsworth Channel avoiding oyster beds, fisheries and other obstructions. Several other drying rythes and gullies lead off the main channel, which give plenty of scope for dinghy exploration at half or high tide – be careful, though, on a falling tide, as Emsworth mud is very glutinous.

The channel divides again at the Emsworth south cardinal beacon, a third of a mile short of the strangely shaped Fowley Island, which is largely made up of oyster shells. The left-hand branch, Sweare Deep, leads towards Northney Marina and the Langstone Bridge and the main channel to Emsworth. This is only deep for half the distance towards the quay and Emsworth

Left: Chichester Channel with The Winner at left centre, East Head on the right. The post in the foreground is the West Winner beacon

Right: Looking west across the entrance towards the Isle of Wight. East Head is in the centre and the extent to which this has been eroded can be seen. The anchorage is at the centre right of the picture

Left: Northney Marina looking north east towards Emsworth town

Above: Chichester Channel with Thorney Channel leading off. The entrance to the Thorney Channel is through a break in the row of stakes that runs from Cobnor to Longmere Point. The Nutbourne and Prinstead Channels can be seen at the head of Thorney Channel

Opposite page: Bosham Channel at high water with Cobnor in the foreground. The stubble fire in the distance is on the Sussex Downs

Marina, where there are 200 berths and which is entered when there is adequate water over the entrance sill. The 250-berth Northney Marina has space for visitors, a chandler, yard and restaurant, and at Emsworth Yacht Harbour the main town is just a short walk away and there are repair facilities, a chandler and marine engineer.

Chichester Channel

The Chichester Channel is narrow but clearly marked between The Winner and Stocker's Sands before widening off the sandy East Head. This is a popular anchorage which gets very crowded in the summer, but care should be taken to avoid anchoring in the fairway.

Half a mile beyond East Head is the entrance to the Thorney Channel, just to the east of Pilsey Island and the least used of Chichester's channels. The main danger is a row of piles which lead from Cobnor Point to Longmere Point on Thorney Island. These are marked by a pair of beacons near the channel entrance and yachts should keep to the left as there is a shoal on the right-hand side. There is adequate depth for most of its length and some deep water and drying moorings but, apart from a sailing club and a hard, there are no facilities except for Payne's Boatyard right at the head of the channel on its western side, where many shoal draught boats winter. Thorney Channel provides a sheltered anchorage clear of moorings.

At Cobnor Point the Chichester Channel divides again, the left branch leading towards the picturesque village of Bosham. It was here that King Canute is supposed to have ordered the sea to retreat, reckoning

perhaps without Chichester Harbour's tides.

There is deep water in the channel to within 400m of the quay and a small pool just beyond the remains of an old causeway. Other than picking up a private mooring with the Harbourmaster's permission, the only place for visitors is alongside Bosham Quay, where they may dry out.

Bosham is a small village with a selection of pubs and stores, there are yard facilities and a chandler at Burne's Shipyard and the Bosham Sailing Club on the quay.

Off Itchenor there are a number of visitors' mooring buoys, and it is not uncommon for yachts to raft several deep on these in summer months. Itchenor is a charming village with a number of shops, pubs, good repair facilities and a chandler, as well as the large Northshore yacht building yard. Opposite is the drying Furzefield Creek with Coombes Boatyard,

Left and right: Bosham and the Quay at high and low water

and a ferry service operates from Itchenor Hard to Bosham and will also take crews out to their boats.

Itchenor Reach is packed with moorings before reaching the two marinas of Birdham Pool and Chichester Yacht Basin. Beyond the Yacht Basin the channel towards Dell Quay dries. Birdham Pool is accessible for approximately two hours either side of HW. The lock gates of the Chichester Yacht Basin can operate at any stage of the tide, though at LW there is little depth in the dredged channel so only the very shallowest of craft can enter then. The Yacht Basin is one of the largest in the country and has good amenities and repair facilities.

Right: Itchenor Reach looking north west

Left: Itchenor and Itchenor Reach with Bosham Channel and the village behind

Right: Furzefield Creek opposite Itchenor. In the background, beyond Bosham, Thorney and Emsworth Channels both Langstone and Portsmouth Harbours can be seen with, in the very far distance, Southampton Water

Left: Dell Quay (in the centre of the picture) viewed at low water looking south west up the Fishbourne Channel

Left: Birdham Pool from the south east. The lock and drying approach channel can be seen at the right centre

Above: Chichester Yacht Basin, one of the largest marinas in the UK. The entrance is locked although the approaches and dredged channel are shallow near low water

Chapter 9

Selsey Bill to Beachy Head

To the east of Chichester Harbour, as the coastline develops towards the high chalky cliffs of Beachy Head lie the ports of Littlehampton, Shoreham and Newhaven and the large artificial harbour created to accommodate the 1,800 berth Brighton Marina. Although less busy than the Solent and harbours to the west and exposed to strong southerly winds, there is, nevertheless, plenty of sailing activity from these harbours

Selsey Bill

Six miles to the south-east of the entrance of Chichester Harbour lies the headland of Selsey Bill with its treacherous shoals extending out towards the Owers light buoy, which is seven miles offshore. The Bill is low lying and difficult to identify in poor visibility, and in these conditions and in heavy weather it is safer to pass outside this buoy than to attempt the inshore Looe Channel. Taking the outside passage adds surprisingly little distance to the passage from the harbours to the east of the Bill when bound for the Solent.

The Looe Channel runs between the Dries Rocks and Boulder Bank about two miles south of Selsey and is marked by the Boulder buoy to the west and the north cardinal East Borough Head buoy to the east. Both buoys are lit. It is widely used by coastal commercial traffic as well as pleasure craft. Inshore fishing boats may often be seen working on the shallows and banks either side of the main channel and craft

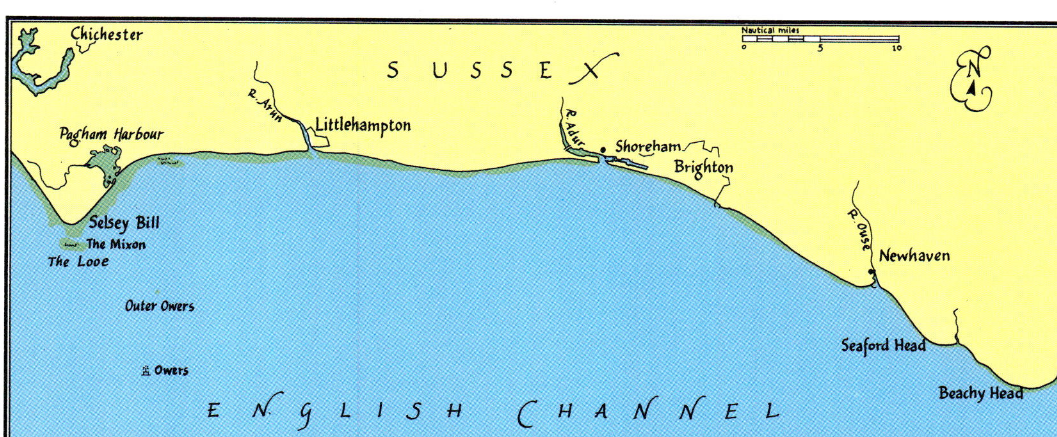

Above: Looe Channel near LW with Selsey Bill in the background. Boulder (green) and Street (red, since withdrawn under the 1989 Navaid Review) buoys marking the channel are at the bottom left, with The Dries and Malt Owers rocks and shoals behind

Above: Selsey Bill, with The Mixon and its distinctive beacon to the right. The eastern end of the Looe Channel passes to the south of the Mixon

Right: Littlehampton entrance at LW. Shoal water over the bar extends for nearly ½ mile south of the western breakwater. The groyne extending from the eastern breakwater, seen exposed here, is covered from half tide but marked by perches and a green, starboard-hand beacon with white topmark at its end

approaching, especially from the west when they have yet to sight the buoys, should not be misled into thinking that these are in the Looe itself. Tidal strategy is important because at springs the stream runs at up to 5 knots and a careful look-out should be kept for commercial coastal traffic. The bottleneck of the Looe Channel results in strong tidal streams even on neaps.

The Boulder and East Borough Head buoys are surprisingly elusive and difficult to identify, though this is easier from the east because of the prominent Mixon beacon on the Mixon Rocks, which is passed to the south before altering course for the Boulder buoy. From the west, once this has been identified the passage is easy.

Littlehampton

At the mouth of the River Arun, 10 miles to the east of Selsey Bill, lies the holiday resort town of Littlehampton with its commercial

Below: Looking south-east across the Arun and entrance to Littlehampton. The pedestrian swing bridge is at the centre left of the picture, with Hillyard's yard just downstream on the western shore. County Wharf, where visitors may temporarily lie alongside while waiting for directions from the Harbourmaster, is on the opposite (east) bank to the Arun Yacht Club pontoons on last bend in the river

and pleasure port. Despite its shallow, narrow entrance which is dangerous in strong onshore winds, particularly against the ebb, Littlehampton is a busy commercial harbour and, in season, is popular with pleasure and angling boats. It is also a lively yachting centre with local moorings, the Littlehampton Marina and active sailing and yacht clubs. The name Hillyard has been synonymous with Littlehampton for many years and it is from this yard that many sturdy cruising boats have started life. Hillyards are still actively involved in the yacht building and repair business.

Entrance to Littlehampton is restricted by the tide. There is a shallow bar which extends a little under ½ mile south from the end of the western pier. Tides also run very fast both across and in the entrance,

Left: Tides flow very fast both across and in the narrow entrance, reaching up to 6 knots on the spring ebb

Above: River Arun at LW. The ferry, which crosses the river just below the Arun YC, has right of way at all times

reaching speeds of up to 6 knots on the ebb. If the entrance is busy, craft going with the stream have right of way over those stemming the tide.

A low groyne, marked by perches, extends from the end of the eastern pier with, at its seaward extremity, a starboard-hand green beacon. This groyne is covered between half tide and HW. When shipping is moving in the entrance all other craft have to stay clear, and when this is imminent it is

Above: The western arm of Shoreham Harbour, the River Adur, can only be used by yachts that can take the ground at LW

indicated by a red and white flag (red over white lights at night) flown by the pilot boat. Just below the Arun Yacht Club on the western shore, a ferry runs across the river, which has right of way at all times.

Upriver and close to the Hillyard yard is a swinging footbridge, and yachts going further upstream to the marina on the west bank (where there are some visitors' berths) should first of all contact the Harbour Office by 'phone or radio or go alongside County Wharf on the east bank immediately above the ferry for directions to these or other visitors' moorings from the Harbourmaster. Just above the marina the road bridge, with a 3.6m clearance at MHWS, effectively blocks navigation further upstream for sailing craft.

Littlehampton has good repair facilities, chandler, fuel and all the typical amenities of a busy seaside town.

Shoreham

Shoreham Harbour, 13 miles to the east of Littlehampton and four miles west of Brighton Pier, is mainly devoted to commercial shipping. Divided into two halves, the harbour runs parallel to the shore with the entrance in the centre. The western arm is the River Adur and is shallow and only suitable for craft able to take the ground, whilst the eastern arm, the Southwick Canal, is entered via locks, open approximately from 3¼ hours before to 3¼ hours after HW. Most visitors enter the eastern, locked section.

Although there is a marina and many local boatyards, Shoreham Port Authority does very little to encourage visitors, preferring to preserve the port for commercial traffic. Facilities are good with repairs, scrubbing grid and shops

within a short walk in Southwick. There is, however, no fuel berth.

The Lady Bee Marina has several visitors' berths, as does the Sussex Yacht Club in Southwick. Yachts locking through into the canal for an overnight visit are charged for a minimum of a full month's harbour dues which, added to the marina fees, makes it an expensive stop.

Facilities in the River Adur are limited to drying berths at the other branch of the Sussex Yacht Club, James Taylor Boatyard (next to the B&Q warehouse) and Pinn Quay on the south side of the river.

From seaward Shoreham is easily identified by the cream power station chimney situated to the east of the entrance. The entrance is marked by breakwaters, inside of which are piers. There is a third Middle Pier on the northern side of the

Above: The cream power station chimney to the east of the entrance at Shoreham can be seen from well offshore and provides a useful landmark. Inshore is the Southwick Canal, entered via locks at the top left of the picture. Between these and the chimney can be seen the Lady Bee Marina

Right: The entrance of Shoreham Harbour looking north-west, with the River Adur branching off to the left. Entry signals are displayed from the white watch house building on the end of the Middle Pier at the extreme centre right of the picture

Top: Brighton Marina is an artificial harbour built between 1972 and 1978 and is the largest marina development in Europe. This picture, taken in September 1988, shows further building in progress developing part of the inner, locked basin into a marina village

Above: Brighton Marina entrance opens to the south-east, the inner harbour being protected from the swell by inner wave breaks and a wave energy absorbing beach. In southeasterly gales the approach can be dangerous owing to seas being reflected from the breakwater meeting the onshore swell

harbour at the division of the western and eastern arms. A signal station here controls traffic entering and leaving the harbour, another signal station at the Lifeboat House at the landward end of Middle Pier controls movement of craft in the western and eastern arms and the locks have their own signals permitting or prohibiting entry. There is also a tide signal, a low light on the Middle Pier (red, less than 2m over chart datum, green 2m—3m, white over 3m).

As with other harbours along this stretch of coast, the approach can be very rough in strong onshore winds on the ebb, the more so as there is shallow water (1.7m LAT) here. At night, although the breakwaters are well lit, they can be hard to see against the backdrop of shoreside lights. There is some tidal cross-set in the approaches, and in the entrance they run at a maximum of 3 knots. Here there are some eddies caused by the breakwaters, especially off the Middle Pier because the stream in the River Adur at Soldier's Point can run at up to 5 knots on the spring ebb.

Entry signals are in accordance with the International Port Traffic Signals (*Reed's* p7, *Macmillan's* p122), and those controlling the entrance are shown from the Middle Pier signal station, whilst signals for traffic in the eastern and western arms are shown from the Lifeboat House.

If prior arrangements have not been made, visiting yachtsmen should call the Harbourmaster on Channel 16 for instructions.

Brighton Marina

Situated to the east of the popular holiday resort of Brighton and one mile east of the Palace Pier, Brighton Marina is a completely artificial harbour built between 1972 and 1978, and is the largest marina development in Europe, with 1,800 berths and full facilities for the yachtsman, from a boatyard, hoist and fuel to chandler, club, pub and restaurant. The marina was originally constructed with inner, locked, and outer, tidal, basins, but over the last couple of years parts of the inner basin have been filled in to create a marina village with shops, houses and flats, many with their own moorings.

From seaward the marina is easily located, first by Palace Pier to the west and secondly by a high-rise block on the cliffs above the marina and to the NW, which has a broad, white vertical stripe on its seaward side. The marina entrance, guarded by the overlapping western breakwater and long eastern breakwater is open to the south-east.

Although, with minimum depth of 2.5m and less tidal stream, it is considerably safer to enter in bad weather than Shoreham or Littlehampton, it can still prove dangerous in south or southeasterly gales, when Newhaven should be considered. This is on account of the effect of seas being reflected

Below: Brighton Marina with the marina village and its lagoon moorings under development during September 1988

Above: Newhaven Marina with the RoRo ferry terminal beyond on the eastern bank. There are regular car ferry sailings from here to Dieppe

off the breakwaters and meeting the onshore waves which creates very confused seas within ¼ mile of, and especially in, the marina entrance.

A similar hazard exists for yachts approaching from the west in strong westerly weather which should give the western breakwater a wide berth. Shallow patches sometimes build up near the western end of the eastern breakwater, so once inside the entrance it is better to stay in the centre of the channel. Apart from this, entry is easy and the inner harbour well protected from the swell by an inner wave screen and a sloping beach designed to absorb most of the wave energy.

There are 200 visitors' berths available, and yachts entering should either call Brighton Control on VHF Channel 80 or tie up alongside the Reception Pontoon (No 10), which is on the left soon after entering the marina itself, and report to the Reception Office which is at the end of the west pier.

The marina apart, there is a large Gateway supermarket, a well-stocked chandler and a Laura Ashley shop – the first of what promises to be a variety of shops within the marina village. Shops and entertainment to suit all tastes are in Brighton itself, a long walk or a short

Left: Newhaven entrance. The Harbour Control Office, from which entry signals are displayed, is on the western side of the entrance, just to the left of the ship

taxi ride away, and buses from the marina run to the centre of town.

Newhaven

Like Shoreham, Newhaven is a busy commercial port, though with a deeper entrance, dredged to 5.5m MLWS, and deep-water harbour it is accessible over a much greater range of conditions. Situated seven miles to the west of Beachy Head and 8½ miles to the east of Brighton Marina, the port has good facilities for the visiting yachtsman with the 350-berth marina and good local amenities. Newhaven is also a ferry port with a RoRo terminal and regular services to Dieppe. Tidal streams are not strong, although in heavy onshore winds, seas to the south of the western breakwater can be rough and confused.

From seaward, Newhaven is easily located by its conspicuous western breakwater. Entry is straightforward but is controlled by traffic signals from the Harbour Control on the western side of the entrance. (Reeds p 22:65, Macmillans p 280) All yachts entering should contact the Harbour Watch House on VHF Channel 16, as local visitors' moorings are limited, or the marina on Channel 80. There are fifty berths reserved for visitors in the marina, which has a hoist, chandler, fuel and repair facilities.

Newhaven is a holiday resort and so in season has a good selection of shops, restaurants and pubs.

Above: Beachy Head and Lighthouse. Rocks known as the Head Ledge extend ½ mile seaward from the cliffs, and in heavy weather Beachy Head should be given a berth of more than two miles because of overfalls extending out from the Head

Index